Leo Dangel

OLD MAN BRUNNER COUNTRY

OLD MAN BRUNNER COUNTRY

Leo Dangel

SPOON RIVER POETRY PRESS
1987

This book is published in part with funds provided by the Illinois Arts Council, a state organization, and by the National Endowment for the Arts. Our many thanks.

Published by Spoon River Poetry Press, David R. Pichaske, editor. P.O. Box 1443, Peoria, Illinois 61655.

Cover photograph by David R. Pichaske.
Typesetting by Rodine the Printer, Peoria, Illinois.
Printed by M & D Printing, Henry, Illinois.

ISBN 0-933180-94-2

This book is affectionately dedicated to my father, to my five sisters, and to the memory of my mother.

Old Man Brunner Country

I

THE HAND ON THE SHOULDER

PASSING THE ORANGE

On Halloween night
the new teacher gave a party
for the parents.
She lined up the women
on one side of the schoolroom,
the men on the other,
and they had a race,
passing an orange
under their chins along each line.
The women giggled like girls
and dropped their orange
before it got halfway,
but it was the men's line
that we watched.
Who would have thought
that anyone could get them
to do such a thing?
Farmers in flannel shirts,
in blue overalls and striped overalls.
Stout men embracing one another.
Our fathers passing the orange,
passing the embrace — the kiss
of peace — complaining
about each other's whiskers,
becoming a team, winning the race.

GATHERING STRENGTH

I looked over my shoulder
at the bedroom mirror and flexed my biceps.
I inspected my body and studied
the body of Charles Atlas in a comic book.

One time, Old Man Brunner winked
and told me how to build muscles —
every day carry a calf for ten minutes
until it's a cow and you're a gorilla.

In the barn, I bent over the calf,
put my left arm under the neck,
my right arm behind the back legs,
and stood up, the calf across my chest.

I marched in giant steps around the pen.
I dreamed about the people who would come
from all over to watch. The headlines
would say: Boy Carries Full-Grown Steer.

But through the dusty window, I looked
hard at the steers in the feedlot,
their blocky shoulders bumping for space
at the feedbunk. I set the calf down.

PA

When we got home, there was our old man
hanging by his hands from the windmill vane,
forty feet off the ground, his pants down,
inside out, caught on his shoes — he never wore
underwear in summer — shirt tail flapping,
hair flying.

My brother grabbed a board.
We lugged it up the windmill and ran it out
like a diving board under the old man's feet
and wedged our end below a crossbar. The old man
kept explaining, "I just climbed up to oil a squeak,
reached out to push the vane around, slipped, damn
puff of wind. I swung right out."

We felt strange helping him down.
In our whole lives, we never really held him before,
and now with his pants tangled around his feet
and him talking faster, getting hoarser all the way
down, explaining, explaining.

On solid ground, he quivered, pulling up his pants.
I said, "Good thing we came when we did."
His eyes burned from way back. His hands
were like little black claws. He spit Copenhagen
and words almost together. "Could have hung on
a long time yet. Anyway, you should have been home
half an hour ago."

HOW TO TAKE A WALK

This is farming country.
The neighbors will believe
you are crazy
if you take a walk
just to think and be alone.
So carry a shotgun
and walk the fence line.
Pretend you are hunting
and your walking will not
arouse suspicion.
But don't forget
to load the shotgun.
They will know
if your gun is empty.
Stop occasionally.
Cock your head and listen
to the doves you never see.
Part the tall weeds
with your hand and inspect
the ground.
Sniff the air as a hunter would.
(That wonderful smell
of sweet clover is a bonus.)
Soon you will forget
the gun in your hands,
but remember, someone
may be watching.
If you hear beating wings
and see the bronze flash
of something flying up,
you will have to shoot it.

LOST SOLITUDE

I have five daughters, who flowered like shadows.
I could have lived alone in my own cave,
but here they are wanting dresses and wallpaper.
Their slim arms harvest in panic every new fashion.

Girlish dreams trip me up; five blank faces
watch every escape road.

Sitting on the evening porch, snatching at mosquitoes,
I am almost back in my cave, when one small hand
becomes a half-moon hanging on my shoulder.

MY FATHER IN THE DISTANCE

You crossed the pasture to the cornfield.
I cultivated toward the end of the row
where you waited in your faded overalls,
your hand resting on a fence post.
Your hand, only once, had rested on my head,
while we stood at the parlor window
and watched sparrows hopping on the porch.
As the corn rows shortened between us,
I saw again man and boy photographed
on glass, framed in the window.

Your hand dropped from the post.
I thought you had come with new orders.
Go home and fix the well pump?
Grind some hog feed?
I stopped the tractor and climbed down.
We talked. Talked about how the cockleburs
were almost gone, how the field
looked greener after that last rain,
how the corn should be knee high
by the 4th of July—important things.

THE FARM KID IN TOWN

My town cousins are Boy Scouts.
Campfires and canoes
beat the hell out of 4-H.
I walk beans, chopping cockleburs.
Town kids see westerns
and hike the river bluffs.

It rains this Saturday,
so we come to town but can't stay
for the movie at the Dakota Theater.
I hang around out front, drooling
over the new show poster,
Randolph Scott leading the cavalry
against savage Redskin hordes.

Then a Redskin my own size stands
beside me, looks at Randolph Scott,
and says, "Hey, this looks good,"
the same as I would have said it,
that wonder and wish in his voice.

I wonder how it feels
liking a show when your side loses.
But the jeans on this boy's slim hips
look wild as buckskin.
I envy him for both his lives, a town kid
and an Indian.

I would go with him and be *his*
faithful companion and sidekick.
We would cheer together
at General Custer movies.

MOTHERHOOD

I wash dishes,
looking out the window
above the sink. The girls,
on the grass, dress
the cats in doll clothes.
The orange tomcat,
wearing a lacey red dress
and pink bonnet,
breaks from their arms
up into the mulberry tree.
His claws splinter off
flakes of bark.
The girls make their voices
sweet: "Here Buttercup,
here Buttercup." Buttercup
crouches on a limb.
The tight bonnet draws
his eyes back, narrow
like slits
in a savage mask.

A FIRST GRADER'S COUNTRY SCHOOL LESSON

He remembers one day from his first grade year. It was winter. During the noon recess, Benny and the other big boys built an igloo in the far corner of the schoolyard. Benny took a candle and a hatchet and crawled inside. Benny's friends rounded up the little boys and made them crawl into the igloo, one at a time. Each came out looking frightened. His turn came, and he was kicked in the butt and pushed on all fours inside the snow cave. He found himself kneeling over a block of ice, where the candle flickered, stuck in a Dad's Root Beer bottle. Benny stood above him like a giant. Black shadows danced up on Benny's face as he raised the hatchet and said, "Are you loyal to Benny?" Say it, I'm loyal to Benny."

He said it, "I'm loyal to Benny."

That night at supper his father asked, "What did you learn in school today?"

SUN GOING DOWN

I'm done, old dog, feeling guilty
that I cut off your back leg
last year with the mower.
You couldn't catch jackrabbits
when you had that leg,
so don't look at me
with sad eyes tonight.
I saw you this morning,
doing just fine with your ladylove,
the Pedersons' collie.
A leg short didn't crimp your style.
I know I turned the tractor
too fast and should have paid
more attention when the sickle bar
swung around, but remember, dog,
it could have been worse.

NO QUESTION

There was no question,
I had to fight Arnold Gertz
behind the high school that Friday.
All fall he kept throwing pool balls
at me in the rec room.

There was no question,
I was scared spitless at the mere sight
of his grimy fists and bull neck.
When we rolled on the cinders
and grappled and thumped each other,

there was no question,
I was actually winning
when the principal broke us up.
And when Arnold went hunting pheasants
on Sunday, everybody said

there was no question,
he was a damn fool to climb through
a barbed wire fence with a loaded shotgun.
There were exactly eight of us guys
who were classmates of Arnold so

there was no question,
I had to be one of the pall bearers,
even though I never liked Arnold,
never would have, but I was sorry
the accident happened,

there was no question,
and if he hadn't got himself shot,
I wonder if he finally would have let me alone.
There is no question,
I wonder about that.

THE BREEDING SEASON

I felt the cold of early fall that night.
The men let me go along to the hog house
to watch the breeding.
Benny had been seeing it for five years.
He said, "It's better
than listening to *The Lone Ranger*."

The hog house smelled of dust and manure.
Fly specks covered the yellow light bulb,
and shadows sat like dragons in the corners.
Merle, the hired man, lifted the gate.
Benny chased a sow into the boar's pen.

Pa and Merle leaned over the pen.
They rested their arms on the top board
and folded their hands.
I turned a five-gallon pail upside down,
stood on it, and leaned my arms on the pen.
I put my hands together and looked at Pa
to make sure I was doing it right.

Merle lifted his leg over the pen,
kicked at the boar, turned him around.
The two hogs snorted, shoved each other
with their snouts.
The boar got up on his hind legs
over the front of the sow. Her head
was underneath his belly. Merle said,
"Whoa, boy, you're getting on the wrong end."

Then Pa was in the pen. he turned
the sow. The hogs pushed each other.
The boar kept climbing on the front of the sow.
Benny named the boar *Wrong End*. "Come on,
Wrong End, do your stuff," he said.

I was cold and tired. I remember
the two pigs fighting again
and streams of dust in the light.
We walked to the house, the men talking
about hogs. My eyes were sandy and sleepy,
but I felt good,
proud of having learned so much.

ONE WINTER NIGHT

A farmer sits on a kitchen floor,
building a toy barn for his son.
The farmer uses wood
from peach boxes and apple crates
because it costs nothing.
He straightens the old nails
and hammers them into the barn,
explaining to the boy
how a ridgepole
will make the roof solid.
There's a blizzard outside,
the kitchen window looks black,
and snow grains brush the glass.
The barn, made of free wood
that could easily split and splinter,
comes together strong
because of habits in the man's hands.
The son's barn on the kitchen floor
has the proportions and shape
of the man's huge red barn outside,
except that, on the small barn,
the man uses some gray paint
left from painting the porch floor
two summers ago.
He explains to the boy,
there is no leftover red paint,
and the boy, because he is the son
of this man,
knows that the logic of a gray barn
is perfect.

TORNADO

Aunt Cordelia was a tough old lady.
We could hardly believe
she was ever a little girl.
She told this story:

We stood on the porch and watched
the gray finger come down from clouds
in the west and dirt swirling up.
Mamma said, "It's over Milo's place."
"No," Papa said, "it's farther south."
My little sister knew
that Mamma and Papa were afraid.
Papa opened the outside cellar door
and herded us in. We stood crowded
on the top steps, watching that thing
in the west. Papa wasn't one to touch
us often, but now his hands hopped
like sparrows from one shoulder
to the next, making sure
we were all there. Even smarty pants
Benny kept his mouth shut.

The tail snaked out and swung around
to the south. Papa became his old self.
The next day, we piled in the car
to go see how bad the Knutson place
was wrecked. Papa said they were lucky
and all got into the cellar.
Benny said, "Pooh, if I got caught
outside in a tornado, I would just grab
a hold around a tree."
Papa smiled, but his face was fierce
and helpless too.
We turned into Knutson's driveway
and saw big trees broken, twisted and torn
out by the roots. Papa said, "Which tree
would you have hung on to?"

THE BOMB LADY VISITS MAVIS MATSON

At first I thought
she was the Avon lady,
same color car.
I was digging parsnips,
the last thing living
in our garden,
a bad growing year.

I let her into my kitchen,
and we sat by the table.
She had a government job,
taking a survey —
did we have
anyplace to go if it
happened? A cellar.
Did we have
any food stockpiled?
Parsnips.

I thought the bomb lady
looked familiar.
Aren't you a Pederson?
My mother was.
Charley's girl?
Marlene's second cousin.
My yes, we are all
practically relatives.

I showed the bomb lady
the crocheted doily
I had finished yesterday.
We talked about ways
to make chokecherry jelly.

Parsnips and preserves
and our fires
banked against winter,
we are never amazed
enough that green shoots
come from the damp ground
every spring.

THE AUCTION

Not even a bid
on the old plow
rusting in the grove.

We were married only months
when he took all our money
and bought that plow —

really all my money, money
I had earned as a hired girl,
babysitting, walking beans.

He didn't ask me,
just bought the plow.
Our first big fight.

His main fault maybe —
if something needed doing,
he didn't think about feelings.

I feel him behind me now.
He touches my shoulders in a way
that says he remembers

how much that plow cost.

COUNTRY CHURCH FIRST COMMUNION

They stood the first communion kids
on the bottom step, the steeple behind
almost touching the black clouds.
Wind tore at veils and lifted collars.
Mothers bent over cameras and fumbled
to get pictures before the rain.
The lightning flash and explosion
came together. Across the road,
a cottonwood tree split down the trunk
to the ground. Out of the silence,
Old Man Brunner muttered, "Ho-
ly shit." The rain splashed
on the gravel. They broke
for their cars, rough hands guiding
little girls in wet lace. The car doors
slammed, sounding cold and dangerous.

II

OLD MAN BRUNNER

OLD MAN BRUNNER'S WALTZ

Old Man Brunner, black hair
plastered across his head,
comes to the dance wearing
brown pants, blue blazer,
green shirt, purple tie.
His cracked shoes are smeared
with Esquire liquid polish,
right over the cow manure.
Around midnight,
some boys, barely old enough
to drink beer, full of envy,
watch Old Man Brunner dance
with a real woman.

Hey, would you look
at that: Old Man Brunner
waltzing with Selma Lund.
Some tight skirt, I'd like
to give her a whirl myself.
See how high he picks up
his feet and sets them down,
like he planned every step —
one, two, three,
with a little dip going into
the first step.
A woman like that, not even
half his age. His breath
must be all whiskey
and tobacco. Still,
the old buzzard can waltz.

OLD MAN BRUNNER SPEARING CARP ON
WOLF CREEK

Early spring, rushing water,
he is out there, below the bridge
at a narrow channel, poised
with a pitchfork. He spears, pitches
huge carp onto the bank,
where they flop and buck until dust
cakes on their green scales.
Old Man Brunner will drive
around to neighbors,
giving away carp from a wet gunnysack.
This is Old Man Brunner's gift,
the flesh of the carp,
his way of almost giving himself—
and there are still those who accept.

IF OLD MAN BRUNNER WERE GOD

Baling wire keeps the bumper
on Old Man Brunner's truck,
the muffler on his tractor.
Old Man Brunner can fix anything
with baling wire:
a wagon tongue, an iron gate,
a split seam in his overalls,
his reading glasses.
If Old Man Brunner had made
the world, baling wire coils
would spark the lightning
in the clouds. Baling wire
would keep the continents
from sinking, twisted strands
would hold the planets
in orbit. Baling wire
would grow like grass.
Old Man Brunner's universe
would be a rusty paradise
where anything could be fixed
with a pair of pliers.

OLD MAN BRUNNER IN CONTROL

Matson's black dog crouches in the grove, waiting to ambush Old Man Brunner's truck. The Dodge truck roars down the road. Old Man Brunner blows the horn. The dog goes crazy. He runs down the driveway and lopes out ahead of the truck, kicking gravel back at the windshield. Old Man Brunner chaws on his WB Cut and drools tobacco juice. "God damn dog." He swerves at the dog, but again the dog is too quick and veers off into the ditch.

Late one night, Old Man Brunner is driving home. He switches on the light in the truck cab and reaches for his pint of Seagram's 7. Coming up on the Matson place, Old Man Brunner doesn't even think of blowing the horn, but the dog is waiting anyway. He charges out but realizes too late that he has miscalculated. Half squatting, front legs stiff, the dog slides out in front of the truck.

The dog and the man see astonishment in each other's faces. Old Man Brunner actually hits the brakes. "God damn dog." The bumper knocks the dog flat, the truck passes clean over him, then skids and bounces into the ditch. Old Man Brunner is down on the floorboards, his shoulder on the gas pedal. The truck roars along the ditch. Old Man Brunner hooks an arm through the steering wheel and hauls himself onto the seat. Old Man Brunner is in control again, up on the next field driveway, back on the road. He touches a gash above his bushy eyebrow and reaches for his pint of whiskey. "God damn dog."

OLD MAN BRUNNER PLAYS HIS CARDS

We play pinochle at Old Man Brunner's kitchen table. The wood box is empty. Old Man Brunner finds part of an old tire someplace and stuffs it into the cookstove. We pour another round of Seagram's 7. The smell of burning rubber doesn't bother us. I am Old Man Brunner's partner. He lectures me after every hand. "Why the hell did you lead off your ace of trump? You knew I had the hundred aces. If you'd played your king, it would have forced Walter's ten, and we wouldn't have gone set by one."

The stove pipes glow red, and in spite of all the Seagram's 7, we worry some. Walter says, "I think the chimney's on fire."

"Deal the cards," says Old Man Brunner. We play another hand. I get another lecture. So far as anyone knows, Old Man Brunner has never made a mistake playing pinochle. I wish the house *would* catch fire so I might say, "If you wouldn't have put that tire in the stove, the chimney wouldn't have caught fire, and the house wouldn't have burned down."

But the house doesn't catch fire. I feel like Matson's black dog, who lies in wait every day to chase Old Man Brunner's truck. I wait for Old Man Brunner to make a mistake. He never does. And if he did, I probably wouldn't say anything. He'd just find a way out.

OLD MAN BRUNNER NAILS JESUS TO THE CROSS
FOR WENDELL AND BERNICE

It started when Bernice found
an old crucifix in the junk room,
except there was no cross,
only a bronze Jesus with the nails
still through his hands,
and Bernice asked Old Man Brunner
to make another cross,
so two nights later he came to our place
with the cross ready for the Jesus,
and Old Man Brunner did a fine job of it,
I got to admit,
with some solid oak, real hard stuff,
from a chair leg,
and I told Old Man Brunner he'd better
drill some holes first
or he'd never get those little nails
pounded into that hard wood,
but Old Man Brunner wouldn't listen,
and he spent twenty minutes nailing
the Jesus to that cross,
and you know how religious Bernice
always was, and I could tell
it was all starting to bother her,
with Old Man Brunner hammering
on the kitchen table, and the nails
kept bending over
until they all broke off, so Bernice said,
let Wendell do it,
but it didn't seem like something
I wanted any part of,
and then Old Man Brunner was going to use
some shingle nails
he had in his pocket, but Bernice
wouldn't hear of that,
said it wouldn't look right, so I found

some tiny brass screws,
but Bernice said those wouldn't look right
either and they didn't even have screws
back in those days,
and Old Man Brunner made a joke
that I don't remember exactly, but it got
Bernice really mad,
but Old Man Brunner finally put the Jesus
on the cross and used the brass screws
anyway, but afterwards he took a file
and flattened out the screw heads,
so you couldn't tell them from nails.

OLD MAN BRUNNER ON HALLOWEEN NIGHT

We breathed the fresh night
into our young heads. Benny led us
through Old Man Brunner's grove
toward the dark shape
of Old Man Brunner's outhouse.
Our arms reached to push against
the back wall, and we fell.
The ground was gone. Old Man
Brunner had moved the toilet
three feet forward. In the pit,
we stumbled all over ourselves
while Old Man Brunner's shotgun
blasted the trees above our heads.
But the worst came later,
when Old Man Brunner told everyone
how he had played plenty of Halloween pranks
in his time and never would have fallen
for such a trick. I tried to picture
Old Man Brunner as a young man.
I could see only the stooped shoulders,
the hawk face, the beady eyes
and bushy eyebrows — Old Man Brunner,
with a sly grin, tipping toilets,
hoisting a cultivator on top
of a chicken coop. Old Man Brunner
dragging a hog up into a hayloft.

OLD MAN BRUNNER'S RUNAWAY HORSES

Old Man Brunner has his road ditch mowed.
He hitches his horses
to the hay rake and heads out the driveway.

There is nothing Old Man Brunner sees
that he can blame for spooking
those horses — maybe a bumblebee, maybe
a snake — but they're off, galloping
with Old Man Brunner yelling,
"Whoa, you son-of-a-bitches."
Old Man Brunner is two feet above the seat
more than he is on it.

Matson's wife is out getting the mail.
She stands holding the mailbox door open,
her mouth open, then dives into the ditch.
Pages of the *Argus Leader* fly up
like a flock of big white birds.
Matson's black dog runs out barking
and is almost trampled.

Old Man Brunner finally stops the horses
and turns them into the ditch.
He rakes back toward home. Mavis Matson
climbs up on the other side
of the road as Old Man Brunner goes by.
"Are you all right?" she asks.

Old Man Brunner says, "I was going to start
down at this end anyway." He trips
the rake, dumping a pile of hay, and says
over his shoulder, "You ought to keep
that dog chained up."

OLD MAN BRUNNER AND THE
   TRAVELING SALESMAN

One stormy night a traveling salesman's car breaks down right by Old Man Brunner's driveway. The traveling salesman knocks on his door and asks for a place to sleep. Old Man Brunner is surprised and happy to find himself in a joke that he has told many times. "You're welcome to stay the night," he says, "but we're short on beds — you'll have to sleep with my daughter." (Old Man Brunner is a widower, and his children grew up and moved out long ago.)

The traveling salesman hesitates. He is actually thinking it over. Finally he says, "Oh, I can sleep in the car."

"Don't you want to see what she looks like?"

"I'll sleep in the car."

"It's all right," says Old Man Brunner. "She's out in the barn finishing chores."

He takes the arm of the traveling salesman and guides him to the barn. Old Man Brunner opens the door and switches on the light. "There she is," he says, pointing to a heifer in a pen.

"I'll sleep in the car," says the traveling salesman, turning and walking off into the rain.

Someone else in Old Man Brunner's place may have hoped for a better ending. But for Old Man Brunner, it is enough. He has a story he can tell to a whole lot of people.

OLD MAN BRUNNER SITS ON HIS PORCH

Old Man Brunner never cuts his weeds.
Right up to the house,
sunflowers and fire weeds
grow tough and hard as small trees.
In the summer evening, Old Man Brunner
sits and surveys his jungle,
his sleeves rolled up,
his cracked shoes beside him.
Old Man Brunner's feet are white,
white as angel feet.
He holds one white foot in his brown hand
and cuts his toenails
with a tin shears.

OLD MAN BRUNNER'S CHICKENS

He'll have an egg for breakfast now and then.
At times he'll even kill a chicken, scald
and pluck it, fry it up, but otherwise
at Old Man Brunner's place, the chickens live
without much threat or help from him. They pick
up oats around the yard. At harvest time
they eat their fill, but mostly life is rough.
Raccoons and weasels get them. Still, a few,
the toughest ones, survive. They roost way up
on cottonwood tree branches, safe, except
for those that Old Man Brunner shoots right through
the head with his old, rusty twenty-two.
I know what Old Man Brunner means when he
says someone doesn't have a chicken's chance.

III

WHAT MILO SAW

THE BELT BUCKLE

There's no use putting it off, Audrey,
I'll tell you straight out,
I can't make myself wear
that belt buckle you gave me.
It isn't true that I have looked
for a belt worthy of that buckle.
I haven't been looking. Audrey,
you might have bought a buckle
with anything else on it, a lone star,
for instance. A horse, a sixgun,
a saddle, a boot, or even one of those
blue Indian stones. But you had to buy
a belt buckle with, of all things,
the Praying Hands. I know
your intentions were good, Audrey,
but didn't you stop and think
what those hands would be praying over?
A man wearing that buckle in bars,
sooner or later, would have to fight.
I ask you, Audrey, would Willie Nelson
wear such a buckle? I hate to hurt
your feelings, Audrey. Maybe
I could hang it on my truck dashboard.

THE DEAD

There are graves in the east forty, out away from the trees. The graves were once marked by a clump of lilac bushes, which Uncle Carl dug out and plowed over. Old Carl kept his mouth shut, and when the neighbors started to talk, he pretended he didn't know that people were buried there, but everyone knew that Carl just didn't want to lift his plow and go around those lilacs. A man from the courthouse and the preacher came out. They said those graves had to be marked. "Look," Carl said, "why not put up your stone over next to the grove? We'll never find the right spot anyway."

"Then we'll have to dig until we find it," they said.

After the bulldozer turned over half an acre, Carl's memory improved. They dug up two skeletons that looked like a man and a child. Carl said, "As long as you have them dug up, why not bury them over close by the trees?"

But no, they said it would be disrespectful to move a grave.

THE NEW LADY BARBER
AT RALPH'S BARBER SHOP

She's in there all right,
cutting hair alongside Ralph.
From California, they say,
young, blonde, and built.
A woman has no business
being a barber, we said.
But soon we saw
how Old Man Brunner walked
back and forth
past the barber shop,
not going in until
somebody was in Ralph's chair
and hers was empty.
In a month we were all
glancing into Ralph's window,
timing our haircuts.
A woman has no business
being a barber, our wives say.
One thing is dead certain
in this town:
we will never have topless
dancers or massage parlors.
When strangers ask
what we do for excitement,
we can say we got a lady barber
if your timing is right.

DOREEN HAS ANOTHER RUMMAGE SALE

I told my Missus,
No, I won't walk across the alley
to Doreen's rummage sale,
even if she is my sister.
Ever since Elmer croaked, Doreen
runs to every rummage sale
in town. She buys chairs
that look like the stuffing exploded,
pans not fit to feed a dog out of,
hats a horse wouldn't wear.
Doreen's yard is a bankrupt
salvage company, and now she plans
to turn a profit on junk no one else
was dumb enough to buy.

Well, Doreen goes into the house
and leaves her wobbly card table
and the cigar box that she figures
to fill with money by sundown.
I couldn't get mad when I saw the Missus
sneak over and put a few dollars
in the cigar box. At least she
didn't bring home a plaster Chinaman
with a clock in his bellybutton,
like last time.

A FARM BOY REMEMBERS

Saturday was for cleaning barns,
forking out tons of manure.
There are more significant ways
to spend a Saturday, when the snow
is melting, but this was ours.
Throw out the shit
and put down clean straw.
Renewal has never since been so simple.

BENNY IN LOVE

Meadowlarks sing around the country schoolhouse. Benny has done nothing inventive for two weeks. The teacher worries. She remembers when Mrs. Himple, the county superintendent, visited the school. Benny made a tiny cardboard wagon. The wagon tongue was a strip of paper glued to the backs of four box-elder bugs. They pulled the wagon right to the feet of Mrs. Himple. But now Benny's imagination moves in new directions. Benny is in love with Eva Hofstader. He dreams about rescuing Eva Hofstader from peril.

Benny thinks about the notorious George Sitz, bank robber and killer, hiding in ditches, underneath bridges. Needing food, George Sitz comes to the schoolhouse. He waves his forty-five automatic at the teacher and makes her stand in a corner. Then George Sitz orders the kids against the wall. George Sitz grabs Eva Hofstader's arm and forces her to collect the lunch boxes.

George Sitz sits in a first grader's front desk and gobbles sandwiches as fast as the terrified Eva Hofstader can open lunch boxes. Above his head hangs the world globe from a cord that goes up over a pulley. The cord runs across the ceiling, over another pulley, and down along the wall, where it is tied to an iron ball the size of a baseball. You can raise or lower the globe, and it stays where you leave it because the iron ball weighs the same as the globe. Benny works his way behind the little kids to the wall. He sneaks out his Swiss pocketknife and cuts the cord. The world crashes down on George Sitz's head. Benny grabs the iron ball, charges out, and conks him again to make sure. Eva Hofstader throws her arms around Benny's neck. Benny lets Eva Hofstader hug him for awhile. Then he ties up George Sitz with the globe cord.

Day after day, Benny thinks through the rescue of Eva Hofstader, refining the details. He feels her chest against him, her face warm on his neck. He smells her clean brown hair. But then the sheriff captures George Sitz. George Sitz will probably get the electric chair. Benny finally starts work on his science project for the county fair.

One morning the teacher finds the smoking remains of a fried mouse in Benny's electric mousetrap.

THE PRINCE

Charlene walks through the grove,
picking daisies. She sits,
leaning against a cottonwood tree,
weaves herself a flower crown,
closes her eyes, and dreams
of Robert Redford on a horse
come to take her away.

Charlene wakes to a clattering engine.
It's Marvin Akerman, the neighbor boy,
on a John Deere tractor,
cultivating corn. Marvin grins
and waves wildly. He will probably ask
her out again. She is thinking
she might as well say yes.

GAINING YARDAGE

The word *friend* never came up
between Arlo and me — we're farm neighbors
who hang around together, walk beans,
pick rocks, and sit on the bench
at football games, weighing the assets
of the other side's cheerleaders.
Tonight we lead 48 to 6, so the coach
figures sending us both in is safe.
I intercept an underthrown pass
only because I'm playing the wrong position,
and Arlo is right there to block for me
because he's in the wrong place,
so we gallop up the field, in the clear
until their second string quarterback
meets us at the five-yard line,
determined to make up for his bad throw.
Arlo misses the block, the guy has me
by the leg and jersey, and going down,
I flip the ball back to Arlo, getting up,
who fumbles, and their quarterback
almost recovers, then bobbles the ball
across the goal line, and our coach,
who told even the guys with good hands
never to mess around with laterals,
must feel his head exploding,
when Arlo and I dive on the ball together
in the end zone and dance and slap
each other on the back.
They give Arlo the touchdown, which rightly
should be mine, but I don't mind,
and I suppose we are friends, and will be,
unless my old man or his decides to move
to another part of the country.

AFTER FORTY YEARS OF MARRIAGE, SHE TRIES
A NEW RECIPE FOR HAMBURGER HOT DISH

"How did you like it?" she asked.

"It's all right," he said.

"This is the third time I cooked
it this way. Why can't you
ever say if you like something?"

"Well if I didn't like it, I
wouldn't eat it," he said.

"You never can say anything
I cook tastes good."

"I don't know why all the time
you think I have to say it's good.
I eat it, don't I?"

"I don't think you have to say
all the time it's good, but once
in awhile you could say
you like it."

"It's all right," he said.

FARM WIFE

The last pan
from the silent noon meal
is washed and back
in the cupboard, and he
is back in the field.

She looks through
the window at fences
patched with rusted wire
and splintered stakes
driven into hard ground.
The dusty trees are quiet
under the force of heat.

She lies down on the couch
in the shade-drawn parlor.
The silence glaring outside
closes around and waits.

BACHELOR

Too much
apricot brandy.
I can see
how I live,
a two-room shack,
peeling wallpaper,
dirty quilts,
rusty sink.
I know the joke
they tell
about the mattress
I ordered
from the Sears
and Roebuck catalog.
They say I thought
that the woman
on the mattress
was included.
But by God,
I might go
and court
Henry's widow.
She might be
my last chance.

WHAT MILO SAW

We worried about our neighbor Milo.
After the hail pounded his corn crop
into the ground, Milo said
he would shoot himself. Milo's wife raved.
She cried into her greasy apron and worried.
Milo's six runny-nosed kids were scared quiet
for a change. Milo took his beat-up
Chevy truck and ran off to town
twice a week and got drunk. Late at night,
on the way home, Milo somehow kept the Chevy
between the fences.

The drought came and dried up Milo's pasture.
Milo was down to his last cow.
He got drunk three times a week and still
managed to keep the Chevy between the fences,
but one night he scraped the machine shed
door a little and tore off a fender.
Milo said he would shoot himself.
Milo's wife hid the shotgun in the cellar
on a shelf, behind the pickle jars.

One day Milo's old watering tank fell apart.
Milo and the six kids dragged an old bathtub
out of the grove so that the one last cow
would have a place to drink.
Milo drove the beat-up Chevy to town.

The next morning, Milo found the one last cow
drowned in the bathtub — flat on her back, legs
sticking straight up, milk bags and tits
sort of floating just under the water.

Years later, Milo told somebody, if a man
was going to kill himself, just show him
a drowned cow in a bathtub.

A FARMER PRAYS

My bank loan overdue,
that tractor I bought
had a cracked block.
Lord, you know
I'd never wish anyone dead,
but when the time is up
for that bandit
John Deere dealer,
let him be showing off
a new manure spreader.
Let him fall
into the beaters
and be spread
over half the township,
amen.

DISCUSSION AT THE WOLF CREEK STORE

"If we went back a couple hundred years, came up
the Missouri River with Lewis and Clark, could we
leave the boat and find the places our farms are on
right now?"

"No landmarks for a man to go by, all grass and
rolling hills."

"I'd find the James River, where it runs into the
Missouri, travel north, say, one good day on horse-
back, look for the highest ground, come back one
mile south and two west. Wouldn't that work?"

"Hell no!"

"Who knows?"

"Listen, if we could go back a couple hundred
years and had any sense, we wouldn't be looking
for the places we got now."

FARMING THE HIGH SCHOOL HOMECOMING

Okay, let's suppose for a minute
that nothing in the float building
and parade was worth remembering.
And suppose we were
fooling ourselves, thinking
that for once we had something
over the town kids because *we*
had the flatbed wagons and the chicken wire.
Maybe there was
nothing original in our themes for floats:
a paper heart and a treasure chest
under the words — TIGERS, THE TREASURE
OF OUR HEARTS. Or a boat
mounted on a flatbed—SAILING TO VICTORY.
Or the theme we really wanted,
which the girls vetoed, a giant crepe paper
jock strap — LET THIS NOT BE OUR ONLY SUPPORT.
Suppose there is nothing really important
in all of that, and there probably isn't
(our papier-mache usually crumbled).
Still, we were never in danger
of believing we could cover our plainness
with ceremony and tin foil.
The warm October wind
always whipped in from the country and blew
the pastel Kleenexes clean
out of the chicken wire, exposing
old manure stains on the flatbed tires.

CORN POEM

I don't mind it so much being a corn-
fed corn ball sitting here by the corn-
crib, smoking corn silk in a corn-
cob pipe, playing a cornet, sipping corn
whiskey, and eating Doritos corn
chips. But where, where is my corn-
ucopia? When will I walk in tall corn?

IV

DRINKING THE MOON

A CLEAR DAY

My field is harrowed and ready.
We eat breakfast while Donna's wash water
heats in a copper tub on the cookstove.
Musty clothes spill from cardboard boxes
scattered around the kitchen.

Outside, I smell bright cold
and bitter wood smoke. I do not fall
on my knees, clutching fistfuls of soil
to my chest. A spring wind chills
worse than winter. Last year's brittle
corn leaves drift over the field
like scraps of yellow paper.

I turn up my collar and start planting
again, pouring oat seed from gunnysacks
into the drill boxes, making that first run
along the fence line, watching
the face of my field change.

DEATH CEREMONY

The neighbors dug his grave,
twenty farmers for a two-man job
and enough shovels to bury death itself.
Old Man Brunner's truck made two runs
to the Wolf Creek store for beer.

The men lounged against tombstones,
chewed grass stems, felt dizzy
in the sunshine. Old Man Brunner kept
saying, "I tell you, you got
the bottom of the hole farther north
than the top — she doesn't go straight
down." When they corrected the slant,
the grave was almost square.
Everyone had a turn at digging.

And neighbors pitching in almost got
the best of death. But one man, then
another, looked away to the south, squinting
into an eye-watering wind blowing sweet
over the waving grass — the last field
of prairie hay in Willow County.

THE WORD MAN

Johnson's hired man came from somewhere, everywhere.
We thought he was an Indian, but his hair was red.
He used strange words that Johnson couldn't even find
in a Webster's dictionary. The hired man's name
was Copernicus Smith, but the kids called him
The Word Man.

Copernicus would say: "The weather looks *larkuler*
today." or, "The tractor runs like a *nukeflee*
this morning." Copernicus used his words on animals
too. They seemed to understand better than people.
He said, "You cats will *wabagatch* when I'm around."
Once when Copernicus was tying up a cow in the stall,
he whispered in her ear, "The bull *grovalates*
when you are in the pasture." Johnson swears
the cow couldn't wait to get out of the barn.

People would ask questions: "What does *slow-waft* mean?"
Copernicus would say, "*Slow-waft* means something like
drawflutter." "Where do you get all these words?"
"Some of them come from the *vu-carple* part of the brain."

Kids liked Copernicus and started using his words.
Arguments started in school: "*Sluseroo* means someone
who is dumb." "No, *sluseroo* is when two pigs kiss."
But the teacher worried. Some of the words sounded
dirty. Benny, the eighth grader, told Alice Bertleson
to go *grovalate* herself.

One Sunday afternoon, the teacher and the mothers
visited Johnson's and had a talk with Copernicus.
Copernicus said that he didn't want to *semepolate*
any trouble. Johnson was sorry to lose Copernicus —
he was a good worker.

THE CLASS REUNION DANCE

I dance with the woman
no one danced with back then
when she was broomstick skinny
and broken out in pimples.
She's beautiful now and married
to a North Dakota wheat farmer.

This is more than I deserve,
her cheek against my shoulder
as we dance
a slow sentimental journey
around the gym, acting as though
we have something to recover.

When the music stops,
we tell each other, thanks,
and we both seem happy.
The wheat farmer frowns a little.

THE RETURN OF SPRING

I walk across the cattle yard,
looking above the mud
at the trees. My boot sticks,
and I pull my foot out.

I balance like a dancer
on one leg, the other leg curved
gracefully, back arched,
arms spread like wings, chest out.

I hold that elegant pose
and watch three crows gliding
around the tips
of branches sprouting buds.

The mooneyed cows stand still,
envying my grace, and I know
I'm never going to get my foot
back into that boot.

BEHIND THE PLOW

I look in the turned sod
for an iron bolt that fell
from the plow frame
and find instead an arrowhead
with delicate, chipped edges,
still sharp, not much larger
than a woman's long fingernail.
Pleased, I put the arrowhead
into my overalls pocket,
knowing that the man who shot
the arrow and lost his work
must have looked for it
much longer than I will look
for that bolt.

CORN-GROWING MUSIC

In that hazy stillness
between summer and fall,
they say you can hear
corn grow. Leaves stir
and sing a whispering song.

I look over my field
and want to conduct
my million-stalk chorus.
I could wave my arms
like a lunatic — louder,
louder, you bastards,
I still owe the bank
for your seed.

I listen again as leaves
flutter down the rows.
Maybe each stalk sings
its own growing song,
as I sing mine, or maybe
it's only the wind.

CLOSING IN ON THE HARVEST

No one could stop him.
A bad heart, he still
worked in the field
and said he would die
on the tractor.
Out on the Super-M
picking corn, somehow
he got off, though,
and sat on the ground,
leaning against the tire,
where we found him.
His eyes were wide open,
looking mean as hell,
like when he was alive
and chores weren't done,
but his hand
lay on his chest, gentle,
making us think
he was pledging something.
We could smell
the dry wind.
The tractor radio was on
to the World Series —
Cardinals 7, Yankees 5,
Bob Gibson on the mound,
one out to go —
the steel corn wagon
was not quite full.

BECOMING THE ANIMALS

He was a farmer who thought
his daydreams were foolish
but he still had daydreams,
and in them
he wanted to be his animals.
He rounded his shoulders
and bent over, shaping himself
like a four hundred-pound hog
in a rye patch, listening,
wondering how a human hog call
would sound in floppy hog ears.
He wanted to be a Holstein cow
who needed his human hands
touching her flanks
at milking time. Most of all
he wanted to be a horse
and carry and ride himself
out of himself and back again.

ONE SEPTEMBER AFTERNOON

Home from town
the two of them sit
looking over what they have bought
spread out on the kitchen table
like gifts to themselves.
She holds a card of buttons
against the new dress material
and asks if they match.
The hay is dry enough to rake,
but he watches her
empty the grocery bag.
He reads the label
on a grape jelly glass
and tries on
the new straw hat again.

PLOWING AT FULL MOON

The air cold,
the hills roll up like unbroken
swells beneath the tractor,
the plow turning a wake
wet and black.

A column of fire gusts
up from the exhaust, the roar
breaks through
finally to a silence felt
in the hands and shoulder blades.

I am with the earth and the dark,
alone. And work is being done.
I'll go home and dream of a horse
bowing over still water in a cedar tank,
drinking the moon.

ABOUT THE AUTHOR

Leo Dangel was born in South Dakota in 1941 and grew up on a farm near Freeman and Turkey Ridge. He attended colleges in South Dakota, Minnesota, and Kansas. He now lives in Marshall, Minnesota, and teaches English at Southwest State University. His chapbook, *Keeping Between the Fences*, was published by Westerheim Press in 1981.

ACKNOWLEDGMENTS

Commonweal: "Plowing at Full Moon"

From Seedbed to Harvest (an anthology from Seven Buffaloes Press): "Death Ceremony"

Plainsong: "Pa," "What Milo Saw," "Motherhood"

Poetry NOW: "A Clear Day," "My Father in the Distance," "Doreen Has Another Rummage Sale"

Spoon River Quarterly: "Country Church First Communion," "The Belt Buckle" (under the title "The Cowboy's Complaint")

A few of these poems appeared in the chapbook *Keeping Between the Fences* (Westerheim Press).

Special thanks to *North Country Anvil* for publishing the following poems in its winter 1987 issue:

"Old Man Brunner Sits on His Porch," "Old Man Brunner on Halloween Night," "Old Man Brunner in Control," "Old Man Brunner Plays His Cards," and "Old Man Brunner's Waltz."